NARCISSISTIC HOME

Surviving a Narcissistic Home and Healing Guide for a Narcissistic Home Survivor

Evelyn S. Wright

Table of contents

INTRODUCTION

In a narcissistic home, the parents' wants are prioritized, and the kids are expected to find various methods to satisfy those desires.

It may seem like there is no help when your family is narcissistic.

Narcissistic parents frequently have a self-centered orientation. They will view their kids as "self-adjuncts," supporting them and their sense of self.

Children in this circumstance rapidly realize that their needs are unwanted. They grow estranged from their true selves because they were raised to deny, undermine, or suppress their innate sense of self.

This weak and undermined genuine self is frequently accompanied by severe shame.

Because meeting a child's needs is seen as being inconvenient by narcissistic parents, they frequently shame the youngster for doing so. The narcissist may come face to face with their own hidden vulnerability when they have a flawed, needs child, and as their shame begins to emerge, they may become aggressive and shameful towards their child.

This temporarily removes their shame and transfers it to the child, who acts as an easy long-term storage space for the parent's unconscious projections.

For young children, the process of shame is extremely detrimental; the younger the child, the more harm it will do. When a child suffers feelings of crushing shame, narcissistic parents frequently fail to offer the comfort and confidence they require for the child to manage these intense emotions. A youngster in this situation will create their own coping strategies, which typically result in the separation of painful memories related to the abuse and occasionally, dissociation.

CHAPTER 1

The Mind of a Narcissist(What goes on in a narcissist's mind)

Narcissistic people are self-centered, pompous, vain, entitled, and unempathetic individuals that annoy and take advantage of others. Although they might not constantly exhibit traits that would qualify them for a clinical diagnosis of narcissistic personality disorder, they are nonetheless self-absorbed enough to annoy and upset those around them. The majority of us understand what it means to be narcissistic, but we are less certain of what causes someone to be that way. What drives the actions of narcissists? What causes them to feel so confident in themselves? We can begin to obtain greater insight as we learn more about what constitutes We may begin to understand the thoughts that a narcissist has and how they support their self-aggrandizing viewpoint.

Excessive degrees of narcissistic admiration are generally thought to be "charming," but high levels of narcissistic rivalry are frequently viewed as "aggressive."

The brutal inner voice is in charge of the critical internal dialogue.

While it frequently serves as a self-destructive internal dialogue that puts us down, attacks, insults, and undermines us, it can also serve as a self-soothing and self-aggrandizing internal dialogue that is also hostile, suspicious, or critical of others. How do narcissists deal with their judgmental inner voice, then?

The majority of narcissistic individuals degrade other people to feel better about themselves. When a coworker gets a promotion, they may think, "He's such a phony." You might get twice as much done as him. Or It's unfair since you deserved more than he did. They can wonder, "Why is he even interested in anyone else?" if they are interested in dating someone. She isn't quite as beautiful as you are. Or perhaps He will pick you! Without a doubt, choosing you is the best move.

It's disputed whether these kinds of thinking patterns result from a more profound sense of insecurity or a naturally exaggerated sense of oneself, but it's important to think about why a narcissist needs to pay attention to these voices.
What would be lost if they disregarded them? What feelings might surface?

Most people who have dealt with narcissism and have expressed an interest in this topic share a similar reaction. If they don't feel special, they can't feel okay.
They adhere to the more binary belief that, if they aren't exceptional, they are nothing. Becoming just like everyone else is insufficient. This all-or-nothing mindset suggests to me that their basic sense of self is fractured at some fundamental developmental They eventually came to realize that it's not acceptable to be who they are. They felt superior for whatever reason that warped their perspective of themselves, but since they were so readily frightened by others, their superiority had to be based on something false or untrue.

People who have narcissistic personality disorder frequently concentrate on their accomplishments and have a strong feeling of self-importance, which controls their interactions with others and decision-making processes. Narcissists struggle to build or maintain connections with people due to their scheming ways and lack of empathy.

They frequently have a sense of entitlement, lack empathy, and need adoration.

CHAPTER 2

Narcissistic Personality Types

Narcissism as a personality trait can be overt, covert, antagonistic, Communal, or malignant. There is only one diagnosis for it in terms of mental illness.

There are 2 types of narcissism when you consider how a trait influences your day-to-day life and ability for forming relationships:

Maladaptive (unhelpful) and Adaptive (useful).

It could be more realistic to think of narcissism as a spectrum with fewer to more extreme symptoms.

The various narcissistic personality traits might then be thought to fall somewhere along that continuum.

In general, narcissism is closely associated with:
 * An excessive emphasis on oneself
* An exaggerated perception of oneself
* A strong craving for praise and attention.

Understanding these and other narcissistic characteristics as well as the many varieties of narcissism may also help you gain a better understanding of the mental processes, feelings, and behavioral patterns that narcissism is known to exhibit.

In contrast to narcissistic personality disorders, narcissism is also a personality trait.
When people discuss narcissism, they may either mean it as a personality trait or as narcissistic personality disorder (NPD)
There is just one type of narcissistic personality disorder, which is a recognized mental health diagnosis. Narcissism is typically classified as a mental illness when it impacts numerous aspects of your life consistently and goes beyond a personality attribute.

TYPES OF NARCISSISM
1. Adaptive narcissism refers to narcissistic traits like high self-confidence, self-reliance, and the capacity to celebrate oneself which can be beneficial.

2. Maladaptive narcissism is linked to personality traits that can have a negative effect on how you relate to yourself and other people. For instance, conceit, hostility, and the propensity to exploit others. This would be connected to narcissistic personality disorder symptoms.

When most individuals discuss narcissism, they often mean the varieties that fall under the maladaptive category and include;

1. overt narcissism:

Grandiose narcissism and agentic narcissism are two other terms for overt narcissism.

The majority of individuals believe that narcissistic personalities exhibit this particular sort of narcissism.

Someone who exhibits overt narcissism may come out as being:

* outgoing
* arrogant
* entitled
 * overpowering
* craving admiration and praise
* exploitative
* Competitive
* lacking in empathy

Overt narcissists are less likely to feel uneasy feelings like grief, worry, or loneliness and more likely to feel good about themselves.

Overt narcissists may also tend to exaggerate their skills and intelligence.

2. Convert Narcissism

Covert narcissism, which is different from overt narcissism, is sometimes referred to as vulnerable narcissism and closet narcissism.

People with convert narcissism don't fit the stereotype of narcissism, which is often perceived as a loud and domineering trait.

An individual with covert narcissism is more likely to exhibit the following characteristics: *Low self-esteem

* Anxiety, depression, and shame

* Introversion

* Insecurity or low confidence

 *Defensiveness

 * Avoidance

* Inclination to feel or play the victim.

Even though a person with covert narcissism will still be very self-focused, this tendency is more likely to clash with a profound dread or sense of not being enough.

3. Antagonistic narcissism

A subtype of overt narcissism, according to certain studies, is antagonistic narcissism. The emphasis of this narcissistic trait is on rivalry and competition.

Arrogance, a propensity to take advantage of others, a predisposition to compete with others, and disagreeability or a propensity for arguments are some characteristics of antagonistic narcissism.

When compared to those with other varieties of narcissism, those with antagonistic narcissism reported being less likely to be able to forgive others.

Low levels of trust in other people may also be seen in those with hostile narcissism.

4. Communal Narcissism

Another overt kind of narcissism is communal narcissism, which is typically viewed as the opposite of antagonistic narcissism.

Fairness is important to those with communal narcissism, and they may also consider themselves to be selfless.

Those who suffer from communal narcissism may:

* Easily become morally indignant.

* Think of themselves as compassionate and kind.

* React passionately to situations they perceive as unfair.

What distinguishes sincere concern for the welfare of others from collective narcissism, then?

The main distinction is that social power and self-importance play a significant role for those who suffer from communal narcissism.

For instance, communal narcissism may lead you to claim (and believe) that you have a strong moral code or care about others, yet you may not be aware that the way you treat people contradicts your views.

5 . Malignant Narcissism

Malignant narcissism is a more extreme form of narcissism, which can occur at various levels of intensity. Additionally, it might make things worse for the person who is dealing with it.

Overt narcissism and malignant narcissism are more closely related than covert narcissism.

Many common narcissistic characteristics, such as a strong desire for admiration and to be elevated above others, can be present in someone with malignant narcissism. Malignant narcissism, however, can also manifest as:

* Retaliation

 * Sadism, the enjoyment of others' suffering.

* Aggression while engaging with others.

* Paranoia, a heightened sense of threat.

CHAPTER 3

Narcissistic Parenting Symptoms

The primary vulnerability of narcissists is shame. They will project their shame onto others, even their children, due to their weakness around it.

All children will seek out an attachment figure because they are predisposed for attachment; they will strive to keep their relationship with their parents and seek out support, solace, nourishment, and validation. But a narcissistic parent is frequently unable or unwilling to give the developing child the emotional validation they require. They won't be attentive to their child or be able to respond sensitively in a way that teaches kids to understand their own feelings since they will be preoccupied with their own needs.

A youngster raised in such a setting quickly learns that their parents find it difficult to handle their emotions and will automatically lose touch with their true reactions and feelings because they know that they will likely be received with animosity.

When a child displays any independence, a narcissistic parent feels threatened and becomes too protective of them. Children with narcissistic parents frequently experience shame and embarrassment and thus have low self-esteem. These children frequently go on to do great things in life, lead disastrous lives, or both. Children who have experienced narcissistic abuse from such parents will need professional help to recover.

Narcissistic parents maintain their position of dominance by selecting a favorite or engaging in triangulation. They may frequently praise one of their "golden children" while demeaning another member of the family. The upshot could be psychological unease, discomfort, and betrayal in children.

These 14 warning indicators could indicate a narcissistic parent:

1. Taking advantage of you for personal gain.

2.Making others aware of your accomplishments while receiving little emotional support or acknowledgment in return.

3.charging someone else for problems that are a result of their own behavior.

4. Making you feel bad for not doing what they want right away.

5. Being admired and important to others but controlling and harsh when no one is looking.

6. Immature and self-centered conduct.

7. Being harshly opinionated at home while putting on a front for other people.

8. Making you feel guilty by bragging about how much they have done for you.

9. Being merciless and unforgiving, doing anything to claim the top.

10. Forcing you to participate in sports or other activities against your will.

11. Not being warm and nurturing emotionally in the relationship.

12. Always wanting the conversation to center on them.

13. Exhibiting abrupt mood swings and explosive rage

14. Triggering anxiety.

CHAPTER 4

Impacts of narcissistic abuse on grownup youngsters

Having a narcissistic parent as a child might have a negative impact on your mental health. These parents are seen as caring and ideal in public. However, they rant, scream, and condemn in private. The parent will exert control over the child's life, be possessive, and see the kid as a mini-me.

Here are nine characteristics that adult children of narcissistic parents frequently exhibit:

1. Adult children of narcissistic parents worry about hurting others if they choose to act in their own best interests. It is challenging for them to think about their own needs without feeling self-centered because they have been "taught" to put their parents' demands before their own. It can be crippling to feel this guilt and indecision.

2. In a psychological manipulation technique known as gaslighting, a person or group subtly sows doubt in the mind of the target, leading them to doubt their own memory, perception, or judgment.

When a parent denies a past incident to invalidate their child's feelings about it, this is an example of gaslighting.

An adult child who grew up with a narcissistic parent may believe that they don't have much to contribute.

Growing up, the narcissistic parent who felt threatened by their child's abilities may have minimized, disregarded, or appropriated their talents and capabilities. Imposter syndrome can develop even when the now-adult has success since they may feel unworthy of it.

3. Even after experiencing falsehoods, emotional blackmail, and abuse as children, it can be very challenging for adult children to stop supporting and loving their narcissistic parents. They might even start dating narcissistic people because they will probably feel bad for trying to set boundaries or withdraw.

They are familiar with manipulative and constrained forms of love, but unconditional love could seem extremely frightening to them.

4 . The parent disregards the child's objectives as they live vicariously through them.
The youngster discovers that their desires and ambitions are unimportant. They strive to win over the parent to maintain their favor.
As a result of trying to live up to the narcissist's high expectations, the youngster may develop anxiety. The failure of the child to live up to parental expectations may result in depression.

5. Whether the parent is overtly abusive or not, they are typically emotionally distant and concerned with their own problems, making it difficult for them to notice their child's suffering. The youngster avoids criticizing their parent and instead places all the blame on themselves in an effort to preserve the family unit.
As a result, the adult kid may continue to accept responsibility for mistakes that aren't necessarily
their fault. In many circumstances, they are used as the scapegoat to maintain harmony.

6. Narcissists and Echoists are complementary to one another because echoists are afraid of becoming narcissists or of having their attention diverted.

In essence, narcissistic parents are prone to sudden fits of rage or tears, which compels their children to occupy as little space as possible to prevent a similar emotional outburst (also fearing taking any attention away from the narcissist in the process).

When a child is trying to do everything to prevent their parent from losing it, it can feel like they are treading on eggshells.

7. Adult children of narcissists are more prone to develop an insecure attachment to their parents and never feel confident enough to be free to explore their surroundings.

A youngster may wonder how safe they will feel in other people's care if their parents are emotionally absent, manipulative, or neglectful.

As a result of having no one else to rely on, some adults become fiercely independent and experience trust issues.

However, it may cause some people to want constant attention from their relationships out of love.

8. Children who have a narcissistic parent will have built their entire identity and personality around that parent's happiness. These children will then grow up building their lives around the happiness of others, with many of them pursuing careers in the helping industries.

9. The parent's actions are erratic. They experience anxiety since they are unclear of what will win the parent's approval. The youngster will feel accountable for the satisfaction of the parents. Additionally, they will discover that parental generosity has requirements, which makes kids feel reliant on them.

Most people won't comprehend the emotional toll having a narcissistic parent has on you.

It will just make you feel foolish to ask for assistance from those who have no experience with narcissism.

It won't compare, even if they tell you about troublesome relatives.

It can be challenging to explain your experiences in terms that other people can grasp.

Children of narcissists frequently struggle with the following issues:
* A low sense of self
*Anxiety or depression
* Other relationships with codependence
*Poor boundary setting
* Trying to please others
* An inability to refuse.
* Constant guilt
* Vacuity.
* A lack of emotional expression or management.
*Trust problems.
* Fury, perplexity, tension.

CHAPTER 5

Surviving a Narcissistic Home

A conflict will ensue if you confront a narcissistic parent directly. A narcissistic parent may experience feelings of humiliation and vulnerability if their perfect world is thrown into disarray by bringing up their undesirable or unpleasant behavior. When interacting with a narcissist, keep in mind that your feelings and perspective are also significant.

Here are 10 tips to help you survive a narcissistic home:

1. Recognize what's going on

With a narcissist, you can never win. You will pay a high price if you do not submit to the demands of a narcissistic parent since they feed on their sense of control. More important than having a healthy family unit is meeting their basic needs. They will only take advantage of the situation if you try to reach a compromise. You must understand that this is not typical conduct.

2. Accept and move on

Unless the narcissist genuinely wants to change, it is extremely hard to attempt to alter them. Embracing their uniqueness will help you feel less anxious. Keep in mind that the hurtful things people say and do to you are projections of how they feel about themselves. These are very wounded people.

3. Reject attempts at gaslighting

A narcissistic parent often makes their child seem insane or delusional, which is unfortunate. Amid a hurricane, a narcissistic parent will insist that the weather is pleasant. The key to your survival is ignoring these egotistical statements and improving your self-worth and confidence.

4. Be Compassionate

The narcissistic parent does care about you, although they may not always act like it. A profoundly sensitive person hiding behind that gruff exterior needs your attention and compassion.

It's time to show oneself compassion after having a challenging upbringing marked possibly by a lack of it. Congratulate yourself for surviving the harsh parent-child connection.

Learn to calm yourself, and show yourself all the empathy your parents were unable to.

The process of getting over such a childhood is not simple. It'll take some time. So, practice patience and self-forgiveness. It's acceptable to prioritize your needs. Taking some time for oneself is acceptable.

If you don't feel like helping others, that's okay too. Saying no without explaining is acceptable.

5. Rely on additional safety nets

Narcissistic parents' offspring may frequently struggle to affirm their own offspring. The trick is to look for other people's assistance. Utilize friends, coworkers, social clubs, and other people to build your own social network. Joining a support group with other people who had narcissistic parents may also be beneficial.

6. Increase your self-worth and confidence

Despite the insults from a narcissistic parent, it's critical to acknowledge your value as a person. Finding activities that advance your knowledge and skills will help you feel more confident.

7. Be Firm with Your Boundaries

A narcissistic parent frequently tests and goes outside of your boundaries only to show you they can. They can unexpectedly visit your house, violate household norms to irritate you or demonstrate favoritism toward your kids. You must establish clear limits and impose penalties when those boundaries are crossed.

You could feel like you are correcting a child, but maintain your composure and be clear about your reasons for doing so.

If they continue to break the rules, you might even need to ask them to leave as a timeout.

8. Communicate Your Plans Openly

With your narcissistic parent, you could feel tempted to engage in covert or cunning behaviors, but try to resist the urge.

It could be best for you to be more specific about your goals and aspirations.

Let them know that you are aware of their unpleasant or harmful activities and state what you intend to do in response. By doing this, you will prevent them from being shocked by your responses and lower the possibility that you may later feel bad or regret your choices.

9. Prediction

Narcissists are convoluted and difficult to understand, but occasionally their actions are expected and foreseeable. By anticipating a narcissistic parent's next move and how you want to respond, you can help yourself cope with them.

Even if you are wrong, there is some advantage to anticipating their next move. Being considerate can help prevent more harm because it's doubtful that their narcissistic qualities would suddenly disappear.

10. Move on

There is a lot of social pressure to uphold familial ties, but these ties could do more harm than benefit.

Give the idea of ending the relationship temporarily or permanently some serious thought. It might be your sole useful alternative in some circumstances. These suggestions are all simpler to say than to implement.

Managing a narcissistic parent by yourself is challenging. Finding a therapist who cares about your welfare is crucial because of this.

CHAPTER 6

Reclaiming Your Power (Healing guide)

All of a person's other close relationships in their life benefit from moving past a narcissistic parent. A child's warped view of reality imposed by a narcissistic parent can have negative effects as an adult both at work and at home. Among adult children of narcissists, low self-esteem, obsession, downplaying of abuse, excessive anxiety, and fear-based responses are prevalent. An individual finds relief by dealing with the effects of narcissism.

The following are the seven steps to recovery:

1. Identify Narcissistic Behavior: Admitting that a parent's behavior is problematic is the first step in the healing process. When something is not acknowledged, a person cannot get past it.

The "golden child," chosen by most narcissistic parents, is pampered as if they can fly. The other kids are regularly made to feel inferior through ridicule, comparison, oblivion, and even neglect.

Occasionally, a parent will change their preference based on a child's performance.

It's important to keep in mind that narcissistic parents view their kids as extensions of themselves, so they take credit for their accomplishments and reject the kids who fail.

2. Examine narcissism: After the narcissism has been detected, it is crucial to educate oneself on the illness and how it impacts the entire family system. Both biology and environment play a role in narcissism. Thus, there is a potential that the family may contain other narcissists or people with personality disorders. A child's narcissism, which is solidified by the age of 18, might be brought out more by the environment. Learn the characteristics of narcissism so you can recognize other narcissists.

3. Complete the Connect the Dots exercise: The difficulty of this next step increases as the impact of narcissism is understood. Initially, it will be simple. Recall many instances from your childhood and adulthood where the behavior was on display for each specific narcissistic sign and symptom. It is beneficial to record these for later use as a guide.

The healing's effects increase with the amount of time spent performing the step. Recall the outcomes of narcissism, both good and bad.

4. Recognize the violent behavior: It's very possible that the narcissistic parent's abusive behavior became apparent during the preceding step. Physical (restraint, aggressiveness), mental (gaslighting, silent treatment), verbal (raging, questioning), emotional (nitpicking, guilt-tripping), financial (neglect, excessive gifts), spiritual (dichotomous thinking, legalism), and sexual abuse can all be perpetrated on children (molestation, humiliation). Trauma therapy is not always necessary, although in some cases it may be, depending on the frequency and seriousness of the experience.

5. Let Go of Your Anger: After the abuse has been discovered and the connections have been made, anger is a normal reaction. It is difficult to understand why a parent, who ought to be loving and compassionate, would act in such a way. Regardless of the elevated perception a person may have had of their narcissistic parent, it is now destroyed. When one parent does not adequately shield their child from trauma, anger can often be directed at the other. Or perhaps the resentment is held inside for not realizing or confronting sooner.

It's crucial to let your frustration out in a healthy way, whether that's through exercise, crying, or talking to a trusted friend.

6.Develop perspective: To get a better perspective, take a moment to stand back from the situation. Start by considering how your narcissistic parents' warped perceptions of the world and people influenced your current worldview. To find the internal vows or promises made as a result of the narcissism or abuse, drill downward. . Use your newly acquired understanding of reality to balance out the misrepresented vows, promises, or images. By taking this crucial step, one is liberated from narcissistic lies and false truths.

7 . Moving Onward: History cannot be changed; it can only be understood. When it is sincere, forgiveness has a potentially transformative force. Always keep in mind that forgiveness is for the forgiver, not the offender. Instead of extending blanket forgiveness, it is preferable to sincerely pardon infractions one at a time. This allows other offenses, present or past, to be understood and dealt with thoroughly.

It's crucial to deal with a professional who understands your experience and makes you feel safe since treatment for adult children of narcissists is particularly individualized.

Conclusion

The environment in which narcissistic families frequently function lacks healthy boundaries and candid communication. It is one of enmeshment and secrecy. Communication will be vague and possibly tangential. People who demand what they want will quickly discover that this is not acceptable. Instead of being expressed verbally, emotions are sometimes expressed through acts of violence or abusive language. Sometimes, addictive behaviors will be used to cover up unpleasant underlying emotions, reducing a parent's availability to their kids even With its concealed traps and explosive emotions, a narcissistic home might occasionally resemble a battle zone.

The non-narcissistic parent will work extremely hard to avoid upsetting their partner while hoping everything will be alright and never really knowing what to expect when they get home.
The non-narcissistic parent frequently suppresses their own feelings and wants for reassurance while avoiding the narcissist in an erroneous effort to control the

destructive rage that might escalate into abuse and violence.

Young children are especially vulnerable to the unpredictability and unsaid tension of a home like this. When exposed to these environments, most kids will develop trauma reactions, including the complex trauma response.

These kids often have no memory of the trauma they have through as youngsters until they become adults. They'll be prone to loneliness as well as despair and anxiety.

Addictions are one method some people choose to cope with their repressed suffering. Others will be left perplexed as to why they find it difficult to trust or connect with others.

These neglected youngsters won't be able to comprehend who they are and ultimately come to grips with the suffering of their past without the help of psychotherapy.

www.ingramcontent.com/pod-product-compliance
Lightning Source LLC
Chambersburg PA
CBHW051938150726
47999CB00006B/2272